Weddings

Paul Mason

Heinemann
LIBRARY

www.heinemann.co.uk/library

Visit our website to find out more information about **Heinemann Library** books.

To order:

☎ Phone 44 (0) 1865 888066

▤ Send a fax to 44 (0) 1865 314091

▭ Visit the Heinemann Bookshop at www.heinemann.co.uk/library to browse our catalogue and order online.

First published in Great Britain by Heinemann Library, Halley Court, Jordan Hill, Oxford OX2 8EJ, part of Harcourt Education. Heinemann is a registered trademark of Harcourt Education Ltd.

© Harcourt Education Ltd 2003
First published in paperback in 2004
The moral right of the proprietor has been asserted.

Editorial: Jilly Attwood and Claire Throp
Design: David Poole and Geoff Ward
Picture Research: Rosie Garai and Su Alexander
Production: Séverine Ribierre

Originated by Ambassador Litho Ltd
Printed in China by W K T

ISBN 0 431 17714 7 (hardback)
07 06 05 04 03
10 9 8 7 6 5 4 3 2 1

ISBN 0 431 17721 X (paperback)
08 07 06 05 04
10 9 8 7 6 5 4 3 2 1

British Library Cataloguing in Publication Data

Mason, Paul
Weddings - (Rites of Passage)
392.5
A full catalogue record for this book is available from the British Library.

Acknowledgements

The publishers would like to thank the following for permission to reproduce photographs:
AKG London/Cameraphoto p. **27**; Alamy Images pp. **10**, **21**; Armenian International (Mkhitar Khachatrian) p. **26**; Corbis pp. **4**, **16**, **17** (Nik Wheeler), **9** (Earl & Nazima Kowall), **11** (Bob Krist), **12** (Charles & Josette Lenars), **20** (M L Sinibaldi), **22** (Natalie Fobes); Corbis/Bettmann p. **24**; Corbis/Eye Ubiquitous (David Cumming) p. **8**; Getty Images pp. **6** (Kaluzny-Thatcher), **7** (Louis Bencze); Humanist Society p. **29**; Israelimages.com pp. **18**, **19** (Israel Talby); Lonely Planet Images (William Harrigan) p. **28**; Peter Sanders pp. **14**, **15**; Reuters p. **25**; Rex Features p. **5**; The Hutchison Library p. **13**

Cover photograph of a Japanese wedding at Meiji-jingu shrine in Tokyo, Japan, reproduced with permission of Topham Picturepoint.

The publishers would like to thank Lynne Broadbent of the BFSS National Religious Education Centre at Brunel University for her assistance in the preparation of this book.

Disclaimer

All the Internet addresses (URLs) given in this book were valid at the time of going to press. However, due to the dynamic nature of the Internet, some addresses may have changed, or sites may have ceased to exist since publication. While the author and publishers regret any inconvenience this may cause readers, no responsibility for any such changes can be accepted by either the author or the publishers.

Contents

Why do we have weddings?   4
Weddings in the Christian Church   6
Hindu weddings   8
Marriage in the Punjab   10
Sikh weddings   12
Muslim weddings   14
Imilchil wedding festival   16
Jewish weddings   18
Buddhism and Shintoism   20
Native American weddings   22
Mass weddings   24
Forty weddings and a bonfire   26
Civil weddings   28
Glossary   30
Further resources   31
Index   32

Any words printed in bold letters, **like these**,
are explained in the Glossary.

Why do we have weddings?

A wedding is a special **ceremony** at which a man and a woman agree that they are a couple. Usually they do this in front of their families and friends. Once the ceremony is finished, the couple are married. Any children that they have will be recognized by other people as part of the couple's family.

Getting married is one of the most important events in many people's lives. It marks a rite of passage between being part of your parents' family and starting your own. Many people only move into their own home when they get married: before this they continue to live with their parents.

This is part of a Hindu wedding ceremony in Kuala Lumpur, Malaysia.

Weddings are also important to the married couple's families. The husband becomes a part of his wife's family, and the wife becomes part of her husband's. For this reason, in many cultures, family members help decide who would be a good husband or wife for someone.

Families sometimes use marriages as a way to join together two groups. For example, in the past the royal families of Europe used marriages between their children to link their two countries together. They believed that this would make both countries stronger.

People entering a church for the wedding of pop star Paul McCartney and Heather Mills, in 2002.

Rites of passage
In 1909, a man called Arnold van Gennep wrote about rites of passage, which mark important moments of change in a person's life. He said there are three changes in every rite of passage:
- leaving one group
- moving on to a new stage
- and joining a new group.

Weddings in the Christian Church

The Christian Church is divided into different parts. These include **Roman Catholic**, **Orthodox** and **Protestant**. Weddings are slightly different in each form of **Christianity**, but the basic aim of the **ceremony** is the same. It means that the couple can have children within the laws of their religion, and makes sure that the children become Christians.

The ceremony

The couple make promises or **vows** in church, witnessed by friends and family. The groom, the man the bride will marry, waits at the front of the church near the altar. Then the bride's father brings her up the **aisle** of the church and the ceremony begins.

Traditionally, it is the bride's father who takes her up the aisle to the waiting groom.

The ceremony is led by a religious leader, standing with the couple at the front of the church. The couple believe that they are making their promises to one another in the presence of God. They promise to look after one another, and to stay married for life.

Wedding breakfast

After they are married, it is traditional for the couple and their guests to have a meal together. This is called the 'wedding breakfast' because it is the couple's first meal together as a married couple. The wedding breakfast does not have to be in the morning – sometimes it might happen at seven o'clock at night!

White dresses

Christian brides usually wear white dresses. These first became popular during the late 18th century. In Victorian times white dresses became so popular that very few brides wore anything else, and this remains the case today.

The bride at a Christian wedding raises her glass happily. Many Christian brides wear white on their wedding day.

Hindu weddings

About 80 per cent of the people who live in India are **Hindus**. Hindus also live in many other parts of the world.

For many Hindus the first step in getting married is for the two families to agree the arrangements. Sometimes this involves the bride's family paying a dowry. This is a payment of money to the groom's family. A wedding date is also agreed, and the arrangements for guests, food and entertainment.

Music and songs

Music and songs – sangeet (say 'san-jeet') and geet (say 'jeet') – are very important for a Hindu wedding. The celebrations are noisy and joyful, and go on for several days. In the days before the actual **ceremony**, the females of both families may get together for a musical celebration. The women sing wedding songs and the girls dance. Sometimes a professional singer is hired.

This Hindu bride is having her hand decorated with henna.

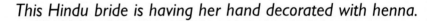

Hathleva

Hathleva (say 'hat-lee-vah') is one name for a ceremony in which **henna** is put on the hands and feet of the couple. Their hands are then tied together loosely with a scarf. This stands for the tie of marriage, which will link the couple together forever.

The wedding ceremony

The bride and groom are seated in front of the **holy** fire. A pundit (religious teacher) leads the ceremony, making offerings to the holy fire and saying religious words. The couple walk around the fire three times, exchanging **vows**.

The bride and groom walk around a sacred flame as they exchange promises to one another.

Sita Bibaha Panchami

This is a festival held by people in the Kathmandu valley during November or December. The people hold mock wedding **processions** and celebrations in memory of the wedding of the goddess Sita and the god Rama.

Marriage in the Punjab

In the Punjab Hindu wedding customs are slightly different from those found in other parts of the world. Once two families have agreed to a marriage, roka (say 'rock-ah') takes place. This is a **ceremony** where the couple and their families get together, usually at the girl's house. Presents are given by both families, and once roka is finished the couple are **engaged**.

Sagan

The sagan (say 'sag-an') ceremony happens on a day that is close to the actual wedding day. The girl's father puts a coloured powder, usually red, called tikka on the boy's forehead, and the girl's family members bless the boy. The girl's family also give presents. Between sagan and the wedding, the two families continue to celebrate together, singing and dancing at one another's houses. One special day may be set aside for sangeet, a musical celebration by the women of both families.

*The couple exchange garlands of flowers. By now, some of the most important people are getting hungry – the bride, groom and bride's parents are all supposed to **fast** for the whole day, until the ceremony is over!*

For the wedding itself the bride is dressed in lucky colours, especially reds and oranges. The groom dresses in a light-coloured suit, and wears a turban.

The boy's family visit the girl's house for the chunni chandana ceremony. They have presents and jewellery to give to the girl. The boy and girl then exchange rings.

The wedding

The couple are married in a ceremony led by a pundit. The couple and their parents go together. The girl's father puts a ring on the boy's finger. The boy's sister then ties the girl's clothes to her husband's. The couple are given milk and sweets to celebrate the fact that they are now married.

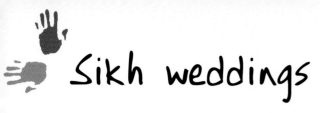

Sikh weddings

Sikh weddings are similar in lots of ways to **Hindu** ones. For many Sikhs, the marriage is agreed with the help of the two families. Sometimes the girl's family visit the boy's to show that the agreement is confirmed properly. After this the boy's family returns the visit, giving the girl clothes, a ring and other jewellery.

Maiyan

Maiyan (say 'may-ann') is a special Sikh custom. For several days before the marriage, the boy and girl are not allowed to go out, or even change their clothes. The gana **ceremony** is then performed – a red thread is tied to the boy's right hand and the girl's left. The lucky-coloured thread stands for a lucky marriage.

This Sikh couple is practically covered in flowers! They are getting married in India.

The night before the wedding, the girl's mother's family pay visits to their relatives. They arrive singing and dancing, and at each stop some oil is added to the lamps the relatives carry. When they have visited all the relatives, the girl's hands and feet are painted with **henna** patterns.

The wedding day

In the morning the bride and groom both have a ritual bath, then go to the temple. The morning hymn is sung, then the couple and their parents stand and sing another short hymn. The couple agree to be married by bowing to the Siri Guru Granth Sahib, the Sikh **holy** book. They walk four times around this in a clockwise direction. The wedding ceremony ends with more singing.

This Sikh groom is wearing a sehra. It covers the groom's face and is thought to be a form of protection against evil.

Muslim weddings

A **Muslim** wedding can be a colourful event. Traditionally it takes place over three days. The first celebration is called Mehndi. **Henna** patterns are painted first on the groom's hands, then on the bride's. Usually these events take place separately, but sometimes both happen together to save on costs. It is usually a time for the bride to have a party with her sisters and friends.

Nikah or Shaadi

Nikah (say 'nick-ah') or Shaadi (say 'shaa-dee') are names given to the actual wedding **ceremony**. First the legal documents are signed in the presence of a religious official. Then the religious ceremony takes place. The groom wears a grand turban. The bride wears a brightly coloured outfit with lots of red, and golden jewellery. Once the religious ceremony is over, the couple are husband and wife.

At this Muslim wedding the groom wears white, while the bride is wearing lucky red, trimmed with gold.

Walimah

Walimah (say 'wal-ee-mah') happens on the third day of the wedding celebrations. It is a great feast given by the groom's family to announce the marriage. Many guests are invited, and the new husband and wife welcome them and mix with the guests while they are eating.

These walimah celebrations are taking place in the UK. The newly married couple will talk with their guests while they are eating.

Jumilla's story

Jumilla, age 17, remembers her sister's Mehndi celebrations in Pakistan:

'At my sister's wedding there were lights everywhere, in all the bushes and trees. We set up two tents, one for the men and one for the women. There was singing and dancing. Inside the women's tent we were able to behave in a different way from if it had been in front of everyone.'

Imilchil wedding festival

Today, in Morocco, some 25,000 people from all over the high Atlas Mountains come to an annual wedding festival in the Imilchil (say 'Im-ill-chill') valley. They camp out in the valley for three days. As well as the wedding festival there is a bazaar, where people sell clothes and other goods. On the other side of the camp is a market, where donkeys, sheep and goats are sold.

This girl is one of the Berber people. She is dressed in her finest clothes for the Imilchil engagement festival in Morocco.

The main point of the festival is to get married or **engaged**. Few people normally travel from village to village in the mountains, so young boys and girls do not get much chance to meet up. But at Imilchil the girls can put on their finest clothes and silver jewellery. There is dancing and music, and by the end of the festival many couples are ready to get engaged, even though they may have properly met only three days before! A **holy** man blesses the couples, and legend says that they will always be happy.

Freedom to choose

An ancient story about a pair of young lovers is told at the Imilchil wedding festival. It tells of two young people who fell in love and wanted to get married. But they were from different tribes and their families would not allow it. The couple wept bitterly, until their tears made two salty lakes. Their sadness was so great that they drowned themselves in the lakes. After this terrible event the local people decided that their children were free to marry anyone they wanted.

The groom (dressed in white) meets his bride at the Imilchil festival.

Jewish weddings

Traditional **Jewish** weddings begin with the bride and groom signing a ketubah (say 'kett-oo-bah'). This is a marriage contract, and is usually signed on the day of the wedding. The ketubah sets out what the duties and aims of the married couple will be. After it has been signed, the groom looks at his bride's face, then lowers her veil.

The wedding ceremony

The wedding **ceremony** begins with a procession of all the guests. Once they have reached the wedding site – either the synagogue or a hotel – the bride and groom and their parents walk down the **aisle**. The couple are married under a special canopy called a chuppah or huppah. They make promises to each other and give each other rings, and then **blessings** are read. The bride and groom drink from the same wine glass. The groom then smashes this to pieces beneath his foot. This tradition reminds Jews of the destruction of the Temple of Jerusalem, and how easily human happiness can be destroyed.

This groom at a Jewish wedding is signing the wedding contract, called a ketubah.

Wedding reception

After the ceremony everyone gathers together for eating, drinking and dancing. This wedding reception is a joyful event. Sometimes the bride and groom are lifted into the air while sitting on chairs. They each hold one end of a handkerchief, and the guests say that they are 'king and queen of the night'.

This couple at a wedding in Jerusalem have been lifted up in celebration of their marriage.

Rebecca's story

Rebecca Gold, age 16, remembers a family wedding in New York:

'At my cousin's wedding they danced a Krenzl, because Abigail was the last of three sisters to be married. Her mother sat on a chair in the middle, wearing a crown of flowers. They played a lively song, and all three daughters did a special dance around her.'

Buddhism and Shintoism

The **Buddhist** religion is most popular in Asia, especially in China and Japan. But there are about 300 million Buddhists in total, spread all round the world. They usually think of getting married as having little to do with their religion. There are no special rites that all Buddhists follow when they get married. Instead, they tend to follow the customs of the country in which they live. Once married, Buddhists may well visit their local temple so that they can be blessed by one of the **monks**.

In Japan, many people still follow the Shinto religion. Shintoism is so old that no one is sure when it began. Its followers believe in kami (say 'ka-mee'), spirits or gods that live in the Japanese landscape. Kami are honoured at special shrines, and people often visit these shrines during or after important events. One of these important events would be a wedding.

This couple in Bangkok make offerings to Buddhist monks as part of their marriage celebrations.

A Shinto wedding is led by a priest called a Kannushi (say 'can-oo-shee'), who calls to the kami to witness the wedding. The couple drink sake (say 'saa-kee'), an alcoholic drink, three times each to seal their marriage. The bride and groom both wear a kimono (a traditional Japanese robe) and the bride wears her hair in a traditional style called Bunkin Takashimada (say 'bun-kin tack-ashee-mad-ah').

Traditional costumes are part of this Shinto wedding in Tokyo, Japan. The bride's hair is arranged in a traditional style.

Yukiko's story

Yukiko Shindo describes some Japanese wedding traditions:

'In Japan, most people have a party to show their husband or wife to their friends and relatives. Everyone looks forward to seeing the bride's dress. We eat Japanese food that has a special meaning. For example, we eat soba (long noodles), so that the newlyweds will get on together for a long time.'

Native American weddings

The native people of North America are made up of many different nations. Some have similar languages – the Cree, Chippewa and Montagnais, for example, all speak varieties of the Algonquin (say 'al-gon-kwin') language. Even these groups have some customs that are quite different from any others.

Some traditional Native American weddings are small and informal, with little or no ceremony. Others have a special **ceremony**, and involve people acting in a particular way. The Hopi people, for example, have a set of rules about how a couple become married. The marriage must be accepted by both sets of parents. Then the girl spends three days grinding cornmeal with the boy's mother (corn is considered a **holy** food). His aunts come and 'attack' the girl with mud, but the boy's mother defends her. At the end of three days, the couple are bathed, then go to the east to make prayers to the sun. Once these are finished, they are married.

Most traditional Native Americans share a belief in some sort of spirit, often called the Great Spirit. The Great Spirit is the source of all life – many people think the sun is a representative of its power. Some Native American weddings, for example those of the Algonquin peoples, ask the Great Spirit to bless the married couple.

Apache wedding prayer

'Now you will feel no rain,
For each of you will be shelter to the other.
Now you will feel no cold,
For each of you will be warmth to the other.
Now there is no more loneliness,
For each of you will be companion to the other.
Now you are two bodies,
But there is only one life before you.
Go now to your dwelling place
To enter into the days of your togetherness
And may your days be good and long upon the earth.'

This girl is having a traditional head-dress draped over her head. She is part of a re-enactment of a Nisqually Native American wedding, in the USA.

Mass weddings

For many people, their wedding is one of the most special days of their life. They are the centre of attention, and all their relatives and friends come to celebrate with them. Other people look on weddings quite differently. They get married in a large group, sometimes with hundreds of brides and grooms getting married together.

One of the most incredible mass weddings ever was based around a **ceremony** held in the Olympic Stadium in Seoul, South Korea in February 2000. The couples were all members of the Unification Church. The Church is dedicated to building world peace through loving families. Marriage is therefore very important to its members.

The Reverend Moon, leader of the Unification Church, in the middle of a wedding in Madison Square Garden, New York City. Roughly 22,000 couples were married at the ceremony.

Ten thousand North Korean couples were married at the ceremony. Rather than travel to Seoul, people had sent photographs to a centre in China. Here they were matched into couples by Church officials. The photographs were then sent to Seoul, and a video of the Church's leader, the Reverend Moon was played. In the video he blessed the couples, and they were then considered married.

Other mass weddings have taken place around the world. In Bahrain, the last in a series of mass weddings took place in December 2001. Two hundred and eighty couples were married in a ceremony at the Bahrain International Exhibition Centre. The weddings were paid for by the Emir, the ruler of Bahrain. 'This is the last of a group of 1000 grooms getting married with the Emir's help,' said his spokesman. 'We aim to help young couples start their life by cutting down on wedding expenses.'

Two thousand couples were married at the same time at this wedding on New Year's Eve, 1999. The wedding took place in Thailand.

Forty weddings and a bonfire

Between the Black Sea and the Caspian Sea lies the mountainous country of Armenia. Armenia has close religious links with the Russian Federation to the north, and in both countries many people are **Orthodox** Christians.

On 13 February 2002 a tiny village called Karpi, about 25 kilometres west of Armenia's capital city Yerevan, was host to an amazing event. This was a mass wedding of 40 couples in an Armenian Orthodox **ceremony**. Most came from Karpi itself. So many couples got married on the same day that the cars that brought them to the church made their own traffic jam, and took 45 minutes to arrive.

Brides and grooms parade around the bonfire at Karpi. They waited for the flames to die down before leaping the embers!

The ceremony for the couples was the traditional Armenian one, and it took place on the 1700th anniversary of the founding of **Christianity** in Armenia. The day was also the day of Trndez, a festival in which newly married couples are expected to jump over fire. A bonfire was built in the churchyard. The brides in their long white dresses waited until it had died down a little before leaping over it. Even so, a few dresses were slightly burnt by the fire.

At the end of the day each couple was given apricot tree seeds to plant. The tree will stand for the start and growth of the couple's family life.

St Gregory the Illuminator was responsible for converting King Trdat of Armenia to Christianity in AD 301. Armenia became the first country to accept Christianity as its state religion.

Civil weddings

In many countries, there are two parts to a wedding. One is the religious part, where the couple agree before their god that they will live together and treat each other in a particular way. The second part of the wedding is called a **civil ceremony**. In this, the couple sign legal forms to register with the government that they are married.

In most countries this civil wedding has nothing to do with religion. If they want to, people can have a civil wedding without any religion being involved. These are usually held in a registry office. They may not have religious beliefs, but still want to be married in the eyes of their family, friends and community. Or they may aim to have children, and want their children to know that they have made a commitment to stay together. Still other people get married at a civil ceremony because they have been married before. Some religions do not allow people to be married more than once, so if they get **divorced** and then remarry, they cannot have a religious ceremony.

Some people will go a long way to make their wedding a bit different! This couple decided to get married underwater, off Key Largo, Florida.

This couple have decided to be married on a hillside, in beautiful countryside. Although the bride is in white, it is a civil wedding, not a Christian one.

Another reason for getting married at a civil wedding is purely legal. If one of the people in a relationship is from another country, he or she would not normally be allowed to stay in that country for ever. But once they are married, the couple are usually able to stay together, and to live in either of their home countries.

Mostly people get married to show that they want to live together for ever. The person they are marrying is very important to them. Winston Churchill, the UK Prime Minister during World War II, showed how important he thought his own marriage was. He said: 'My most brilliant achievement was my ability to be able to persuade my wife to marry me.'

Glossary

aisle walkway or path between two rows of seats

blessing gift from God or a holy person. The gift can be real or it can be imagined: for example, a priest wishing a newly married couple a happy future would be giving them a blessing.

ceremony a special ritual and celebration

Christians (Christianity) people who follow the religion of Christianity, which is based on the teachings of Jesus Christ. Christians believe that Jesus was the Son of God.

civil ceremony non-religious marriage ceremony in which the couple sign papers to show that they are legally married

divorce legal end of a marriage, after a period of separation

engaged term that describes a couple who have announced that they plan to be married

henna extract of a plant root, which is often used to dye skin or hair a reddish-brown colour

Hindus (Hinduism) people who follow Hinduism. Hindus worship one god (called Brahman) in many forms. Hinduism is the main religion in India.

holy special because it is to do with God or a religious purpose

Jews (Judaism) people who follow the religion of Judaism. Jews pray to one god. Their holy book is the Hebrew Bible, sometimes called the Old Testament by Christians.

monk member of a monastery, an all-male religious community. Monks devote their lives to God.

Muslims (Islam) people who follow the religion of Islam. Muslims pray to one god, whom they call Allah.

Orthodox strict or 'traditional'. Orthodox Christians originally came from eastern and south-eastern Europe. Their part of the Christian church divided from Roman Catholicism hundreds of years ago.

Protestants people who believe in a form of Christianity that began in Germany in the 16th century, when Christianity first broke away from the Pope's leadership

Roman Catholics Christians who follow the leadership of the Pope in Rome

Sikhs (Sikhism) people who follow the religion of Sikhism, based on the teachings of the ten Gurus, or teachers

vows promises made according to a special set of rules for a particular ceremony

Further resources

More books to read
Religions of the World (series), Sue Penney (Heinemann Library, 2002)

(Un)arranged Marriage, Bali Rai (Corgi Juvenile, 2001)

Wedding Days, Anita Ganeri (Evans Brothers, 1998)

Websites
www.weddingworld.co.za/resource/feature_articles/culture.htm
Looks at wedding traditions around the world.

www.church-weddings.co.uk
Looks at how wedding ceremonies are carried out within different religions

Index

Armenian weddings 26–7

blessings 17, 18, 20, 23, 25
brides 6, 7, 9, 10, 11, 13, 14, 18, 19, 21, 27
Buddhism 20

ceremonies 4, 6, 9, 10–11, 12, 13, 14, 18, 22
choosing a partner 5
Christian weddings 6–7, 26–7
civil weddings 28–9
clothes 7, 11, 14, 17, 21

divorce 28
dowries 8

engagement 10, 17

family ties 5
flower garlands 10, 11

grooms 6, 9, 10, 11, 13, 14, 18, 19, 21

Hathleva 9
henna patterns 9, 13, 14
Hindu weddings 8–9

Imilchil wedding festival 16–17

Jewish weddings 18–19

Maiyan 12
marriage contracts 18
mass weddings 24–7
meals and special foods 7, 15, 19, 21
Mehndi 14, 15
Moroccan weddings 16–17
music and dance 8, 10, 13, 15, 17, 19
Muslim weddings 14–15

Native American weddings 22–3
Nikah 14

presents 10, 11, 12
Punjab weddings 10–11

rings 11, 12
rites of passage 4, 5
royal marriages 5

Sagan 10
Shaadi 14
Shinto weddings 20–1
Sikh weddings 12–13
Sita Bibaha Panchami 9

Unification Church weddings 24–5

vows 6, 9, 18

Walimah 15
wedding breakfasts 7